WORLD of TECHNOLOGY

THIS EDITION
Editorial Management by Oriel Square
Produced for DK by WonderLab Group LLC
Jennifer Emmett, Erica Green, Kate Hale, *Founders*

Editors Grace Hill Smith, Libby Romero, Maya Myers, Michaela Weglinski;
Photography Editors Kelley Miller, Annette Kiesow, Nicole DiMella; **Managing Editor** Rachel Houghton;
Designers Project Design Company; **Researcher** Michelle Harris; **Copy Editor** Lori Merritt;
Indexer Connie Binder; **Proofreader** Larry Shea; **Reading Specialist** Dr. Jennifer Albro;
Curriculum Specialist Elaine Larson

Published in the United States by DK Publishing
1745 Broadway, 20th Floor, New York, NY 10019

Copyright © 2023 Dorling Kindersley Limited
DK, a Division of Penguin Random House LLC
23 24 25 26 10 9 8 7 6 5 4 3 2 1
001-334102-July/2023

All rights reserved.

Without limiting the rights under the copyright reserved above, no part of this publication may be reproduced, stored in or introduced into a retrieval system, or transmitted, in any form, or by any means (electronic, mechanical, photocopying, recording, or otherwise), without the prior written permission of the copyright owner.
Published in Great Britain by Dorling Kindersley Limited

A catalog record for this book
is available from the Library of Congress.
HC ISBN: 978-0-7440-7469-7
PB ISBN: 978-0-7440-7470-3

DK books are available at special discounts when purchased in bulk for sales promotions, premiums,
fundraising, or educational use. For details, contact: DK Publishing Special Markets,
1745 Broadway, 20th Floor, New York, NY 10019
SpecialSales@dk.com

Printed and bound in China

The publisher would like to thank the following for their kind permission to reproduce their images:
a=above; c=center; b=below; l=left; r=right; t=top; b/g=background

123RF.com: Dmitry Azarov 29tr, Sergey Peterman 11tr; **Alamy Stock Photo:** imageBROKER / Heiner Heine 34tl, Independent Picture Service / Todd Strand 15bl, Sergii Iaremenko / Science Photo Library 39tr, Jochen Tack 24tl, ZUMA Press Inc / Howard Lipin / San Diego Union-Tribune 25tr; **Dreamstime.com:** Piotr Adamowicz 26br, Alhovik 17tr, Daria Amoseeva 27tr, Sorrapong Apidech 24-25, Yuri Arcurs 18tl, Sven Bachstroem 43tr, Andrew Barker 9bl, Beijing Hetuchuangyi Images Co., Ltd., 38-39b, Katarzyna Bialasiewicz 24cl, Alexandr Blinov 6tl, Bluebay2014 12-13b, Bluetoes67 26clb, Dark1elf 32-33t, David A Dodson 10clb, Dragoscondrea 21tr, Ekkasit919 28tl, 35tr, Elenanoeva 21crb, Eskymaks 40cl, Paolo De Gasperis 20t, Florin Ghidu 44clb, Gall Gusztv / Gallofoto 9tr, Info849943 26tl, Jamesteohart 16tl, Jhwhverdonk 44-45t, Kittipong Jirasukhanont 28br, Khoamartin 31tr, Maksim Laptanovich 10tl, Larysole 8tl, Pratchaya Leelapatchayanont 23tr, Lightpoet 30-31b, Ekachai Lohacamonchai 12tl, Pop Nukoonrat 6-7b, Vudhikul Ocharoen 21bl, Evgeniy Parilov 37tr, Peuceta 45tr, Andrey Popov 33tr, 38tl, Pricelessphotos 15bc, Prostockstudio 1cb, Alexander Raths 32tl, Rattanachot2525 30tl, Rido 22-23b, Robertax 29l, Scharfsinn86 34-35b, Golden Sikorka 40-41b, Anton Starikov / Coprid 27bl, Syda Productions / Dolgachov 3cb, Veerapong Takonok 14clb, Tashka2000 22tlb, U96 25bl, Unpict 37cr, Volodymyrkrasyuk 41tr, Wavebreakmedia Ltd 10r, 14r, Xxzoexx 4-5, Yadamons 36-37b, Hongqi Zhang (aka Michael Zhang) 17bl; **Getty Images:** Science & Society Picture Library 7tr, Stone / John M Lund Photography Inc 18cl; **Getty Images / iStock:** E+ / kali9 18-19b; **NASA:** 7tr, JPL-Caltech 42tl, JPL-Caltech / MSSS 43bl; **Shutterstock.com:** CC Photo Labs 20cla, Yauhen_D 40tl

Cover images: *Front:* **Dreamstime.com:** Sdecoret, *Back:* **Shutterstock.com:** Vector Tradition cra, Vector_dream_team cla

All other images © Dorling Kindersley
For more information see: www.dkimages.com

For the curious
www.dk.com

WORLD of TECHNOLOGY

Roxanne Troup

CONTENTS

6	What Is Technology?
8	Technology and Communication
16	News and Entertainment
22	Tech for Work and School
26	A Helpful House
28	Medical Technology

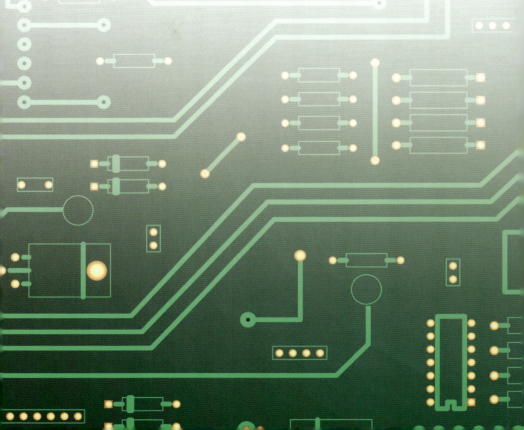

34 Agricultural Technology

38 Technology and Transportation

42 Exploring with Technology

46 Glossary

47 Index

48 Quiz

WHAT IS TECHNOLOGY?

We use technology every day. But what is technology? If you said, "Technology is a computer, tablet, or smartphone," you would be right. But technology is so much more than electronics. Technology is the practical use of science. Computers, vaccines, and even the wheel are all kinds of technology. In fact, any invention or discovery that makes life better is technology!

The First Wheel
The first wheel was created in 3500 BCE to make pottery.

What's in a Name?
The word "technology" comes from two Greek words: *technē*, which means "art or skill," and *logos*, which means "word or speech." It originally meant to "talk about art."

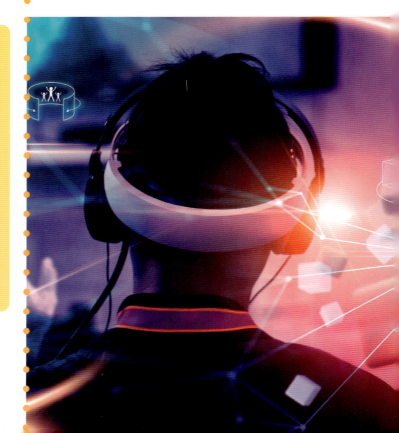

Now, more than ever, technology affects every area of our lives. It helps us communicate with far-off family. It gives us access to news and entertainment when we want it. Technology makes work, school, and chores easier to do. It keeps us healthy and safe. It even improves the way we grow our food. Technology is everywhere!

Programming Pioneer
Some people consider Ada King, the countess of Lovelace, to be the first computer programmer. In 1843, the English mathematician wrote programs, or step-by-step instructions, for the first mechanical computer.

Going Electric
The first all-electric computer was built during World War II. It was so large it could have filled a shipping container!

Connected by Wire
To send a telegraph, operators sent coded messages over a wire using Morse code. In Morse code, each letter of the alphabet is represented by a combination of long and short sounds called dashes and dots.

Different Lengths
Radio waves can be as short as the tip of your pencil or more than 62 miles (100 km) long!

TECHNOLOGY AND COMMUNICATION

The technology people use to communicate today wouldn't be possible without Heinrich Hertz. In the late 1800s, this German scientist discovered radio waves while studying the relationship between electricity and magnetism. Radio waves are invisible, electromagnetic waves. They travel at the speed of light and carry information.

Hertz did not realize how important radio waves would become. But they have transformed the way people communicate. Before Hertz's discovery, people used telegraphs and telephones for long distance communication. Messages traveled along wires, one house or building at a time. Radio waves allowed communication to go wireless. Using them, messages could travel faster and farther than ever before.

Today, lots of different technologies rely on radio waves. Radios, computers, cell phones, televisions, satellites, and GPS devices all use radio waves to send and receive information.

Early Calls
The American Telephone and Telegraph Company (AT&T) was founded in 1885. It was one of the first telephone companies in the United States.

Amazing Radio Waves
Radio waves can travel through objects and space. The National Aeronautics and Space Administration (NASA) uses radio waves to find and study objects in space. The waves are used to find far-off galaxies.

9

Unique Signals
Cell phones broadcast using different frequencies to keep phone calls from getting mixed up in the air.

Out with the Old
Most people now own cell phones. They don't have a landline. So, many telephone companies want to remove telephone wires and focus on wireless technology.

So, exactly how does a cell phone use radio waves? When you use a cell phone, a tiny computer inside it changes the sound of your voice or the words in your text into binary code. Binary code is an electric signal made up of zeros and ones that computers read. The phone transmits, or sends, that signal on a radio wave. A nearby cell tower picks up the signal and passes it to a switcher. Inside the switcher, another computer reads the signal. It then searches for the right place to send the information—your friend's phone.

The switcher repackages your call into another radio wave and sends it to a cell tower near your friend. A receiver inside your friend's phone catches the signal and changes it back to its original form. If your friend is on a landline, the switcher passes the signal through the phone lines going into your friend's home.

Smartphones
The first cell phones were more like walkie-talkies than computers. They could only send and receive calls. Today, most cell phones are "smart." Smartphones are small computers that can connect to the internet, make calls, and send texts. Over six billion people in the world own a smartphone.

You've Got Mail!
The word "email" is short for electronic mail.

People communicate with computers, too. On their own, computers can only process and store information. But connected to a network, or a group of computers, a computer can share information with any other computer on the network.

The internet is a huge network. It was developed to connect computers in different places and allow them to share information.

Connecting the World
Five billion people have access to the internet.

People access the internet in many different ways—on smartphones, tablets, or any computer linked to the network. Once on the internet, an endless supply of information becomes available. You can discover when your favorite movie is playing or learn about sharks. You can buy a new pair of shoes, send an email, or connect with friends around the world.

The internet connects computers using both wires and radio waves. Wireless internet is called Wi-Fi.

Email Fun Facts
In 1971, a computer engineer named Ray Tomlinson sent the first email. He sent it to himself. Twenty years later, NASA astronauts sent the first email from space. It said, "Hello, Earth!" Today, over 3.5 million emails are sent each second.

13

Search Engines

Do you want to learn about puppies? Just type "puppies" into your internet search bar. A search engine like Google will use the key words you type to help you find information quickly.

Constantly Searching

Google receives about 8.5 billion search requests every day.

14

Information on the internet is hosted on the World Wide Web. The web is like a library full of books. Each "book" is a website with multiple pages of information. Just like each book in a library has its own call numbers, each website has its own address. Web addresses are known as uniform resource locators, or URLs. They track where a website is stored on the internet. Many URLs start with "www" to show they are located on the World Wide Web.

Computers connected to the internet have their own addresses. Computer addresses are called internet protocol, or IP, addresses. An IP address is a string of numbers and periods that tell the network which computer is connecting to it.

What's in a Name?
People use different words to describe the internet. In the 1990s, people were amazed at the internet's speed. They called it an information superhighway. Today, people compare the internet to the vastness of space. They call it cyberspace.

call numbers

webpage URL

15

NEWS AND ENTERTAINMENT

"Extra! Extra! Read all about it!" In the past, those words were a call to everyone within listening distance that something big had just happened—and the local newspaper had the latest scoop.

Technology has changed the way we consume news. Before the development of internet and cable television, news was reported at specific times. Some newspapers were published once or twice a day. Others came out once a week. Television stations reported news in the morning, at noon, and at night. Occasionally, a special report would interrupt a show, but breaking news was often first reported on the radio. Today, we get those same kinds of updates on a banner that scrolls across our TV screens or from alerts on our phones.

History of Television
The first TV station began broadcasting in 1928—all in black-and-white. The first color TV was sold in 1954. The first TV commercial aired during a baseball game between the Brooklyn Dodgers and Philadelphia Phillies in 1941.

Going to the Movies
Movies have been around for nearly 100 years. Since then, filmmakers have added sound, color, and lots of different special effects to create the "movie magic" we see today.

Technology has also had a big impact on entertainment. Just a few decades ago, a limited number of TV stations broadcast a limited number of shows. If you missed your favorite show, too bad. To see a movie, you went to the theater. To hear music, you went to a concert, turned on the radio, or bought a record. Today, news and entertainment are available anytime, anywhere on all kinds of different devices.

Attention!
"Breaking News" is considered to be so important that it can interrupt or "break in" on another show.

Digital News
Every major newspaper in the world has a digital edition posted online. Today, *The New York Times* publishes an average of 200 news stories every day—in print, digital, audio, and visual formats.

Smile!
Every day, 3.2 billion photos are shared on social media.

Fake News
Fake news stories try to find readers—and make money—by sharing wild conspiracy theories and false news instead of facts. They are often found online.

Thanks to the internet, you can now access nearly any type of content you desire. People use the internet to download music, stream movies and TV shows, read e-books, and download books from the library. They also listen to podcasts. Podcasts are like radio talk shows that offer new content on a regular basis. Some podcasts record interviews or audio stories, while others offer educational content to enjoy whenever you like.

But not everything posted online is true. The internet is an open-source network. That means anyone can add to it or change it without asking for permission. This is both good and bad. Open-source technologies let people work together to make improvements. But there are no global gatekeepers outlining how those technologies should be used. So, people can post anything they want online—even if it is dangerous or untrue.

Evaluating Content
It's important for people to think critically about what they see online. To do that, consider where the information comes from. Check to see how old the information is. Think about why someone might have posted the content. Then, compare the information to resources that you trust.

Most smart TVs come preloaded with streaming apps.

More Smart Devices

Any device that connects to the internet is a smart device. These objects are part of the Internet of Things, or IoT. Appliances, doorbell cameras, and automatic lights controlled from a smartphone are all IoTs.

Smart TVs are another kind of technology that has changed how people consume news and entertainment. Smart TVs aren't super brainy. They're just really connected. Smart TVs use Wi-Fi to connect to other devices on a network. A smart TV connects to online streaming services so people can watch movies and television shows. On a streaming service, shows are available any time or place. People can even pause and rewind them while they watch!

20

Smart TVs don't just stream content. They can also pick up broadcast stations with an antenna or cable service. And they have special ports or plug-ins to connect directly to video game systems and devices without Wi-Fi.

Virtual reality (VR) takes the viewing experience a step further. VR uses computer technology to create a 3D world for users to explore. VR headsets are like goggles that block out the real world. They use sound—and sometimes smell—to make users think they're in the virtual world. Some VR devices even have gloves to mimic the sense of touch.

TV ports

Virtual Training
Virtual reality can be used for education and job training. Architects and engineers use VR to view models of their designs. Medical students use virtual reality to practice caring for patients.

Another Wireless Option
Bluetooth connects devices wirelessly, but it is designed to travel over short distances.

21

Help Wanted
Sometimes, businesses rely on technology to find employees. They post job openings online. People send their resumes by email or complete applications online.

TECH FOR WORK AND SCHOOL

Technology is especially useful at work. It helps businesses track money, make schedules, and create presentations. It also allows people to collaborate, or work together, even when they work from home.

Businesses rely on technology to connect with and care for their customers. Often, first contact is made online through the store's website. But that's just a tiny piece of the technology that stores use when someone goes shopping.

QR Codes
A QR code works just like a barcode. It is just a different shape.

Every product in a store has a unique barcode or QR code on its packaging. The codes may look the same, but each one is unique and packed with information.

When a clerk scans a barcode or QR code on a package, a computer removes that item from the store's number of items in stock. Store managers track this information. It tells them when to reorder products for their store.

Telecommuting
People who work from home use portable, or moveable, technologies like laptops and smartphones. With an internet connection, any space can become a workplace.

Barcodes
Barcodes help businesses track the products on their shelves.

23

Tech for Virtual Classrooms
In virtual classrooms, teachers link to documents, videos, and other internet resources to help students learn from anywhere.

Tech in the Classroom
Interactive whiteboards connect to a computer and work like a touchscreen monitor. Students can write, draw, and move objects on the screen with a finger. Students can share their learning with the entire class.

Technology is also helpful at school. Schools have used computers to help students in the classroom for decades. Computers help students research and write reports, practice math skills, and learn to type and code. But in 2020, things changed. A quick-spreading coronavirus called COVID-19 caused schools and businesses around the world to close.

Computers came to the rescue! Teachers created virtual classrooms so their students could continue learning. They posted lessons and assignments online. Teachers connected with their students over live video and even took their classes on virtual field trips. Online platforms allowed students to collaborate with classmates, read online textbooks, and even welcome guest speakers—like authors and scientists!

Making Learning Fun
Programmable robots are a fun way to learn how to code. Using an app, users input step-by-step instructions for the robot to follow.

A HELPFUL HOUSE

People use all sorts of technology in their homes. Programmable thermostats keep homes cool in the summer and warm in winter. Sensors can turn lights on and off based on the time of day. Robots can even help clean! Shaped like big hockey pucks, some robots can be programmed to vacuum the floor. When the job is done, the robots return to their charging stations to prepare for the next scheduled cleaning.

Virtual Help
Virtual assistants recognize speech. Just call out their name and ask a question or tell them what to do.

In the Yard
A robotic lawn mower can be programmed to cut the grass.

Virtual assistants like Alexa or Google Home keep people organized. These devices connect to the internet and smartphones. They keep track of appointments and remind people when it's time to do things like take medicine or walk the dog. Virtual assistants can make shopping lists and place orders online. They can also play music, help with homework, and tell jokes.

Some homes are smart homes. Their lights, locks, thermostats, and appliances can be controlled remotely with a phone or computer. If a home has a virtual assistant, it can control everything connected to the system.

Spotless View
This robot sticks to windows. As sensors guide it up and down, it sprays and wipes the window clean.

Better Light Bulbs
The first light-emitting diode (LED) lightbulb was invented in 1962. Over the past few decades, LED lights have become brighter and more reliable. Today, LEDs are used in homes, offices, hospitals, and schools.

Hospital Robots
Some hospitals and doctors' offices use robots to help with routine tasks like making deliveries, restocking supplies, and checking patients in.

MEDICAL TECHNOLOGY

Technology makes life-saving differences in medicine. Medical technology includes many things. VR technology trains medical students to recognize health issues and do procedures. At-home devices check people's blood sugar. There are also robots that help keep hospitals clean. Even the GPS technology first responders use to control traffic lights in an emergency—turning the light green so ambulances can safely pass through—is medical technology.

Robots even helps doctors perform surgery. Doctors control its robotic arms with a computer while tiny cameras give the doctors a close-up 3D view of what the robot is doing.

Healing Time
Robotic-assisted surgery requires just a few small cuts, so patients recover faster.

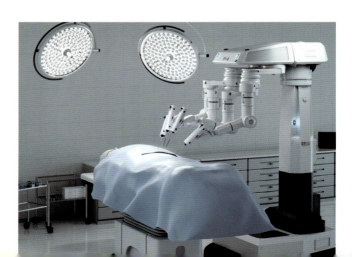

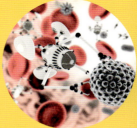

Developing Tech
Someday, microscopic robots called nanobots could be injected into your bloodstream. Nanobots may help doctors find and treat diseases like cancer before they can harm your body. But right now, they are still being tested.

Super Cleaners
These robots use ultraviolet (UV) light to keep busy places like hospitals and airports clean. They roll into a hospital room and shine a UV light that kills germs.

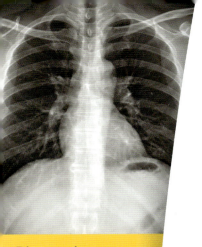

Have you ever broken a bone? If so, you probably had an X-ray. X-rays have been around for a long time. They use high-energy light waves to "see" inside your body. As the X-ray beam passes through, some of the rays are absorbed by your bones. Light that isn't absorbed creates a gray, shadowy image on a black film. In places where light is absorbed, a white image appears. This makes it easy for doctors to see broken bones. They look white on the film.

Discovering X-rays
German physicist Wilhelm Roentgen accidently discovered X-rays in 1895. He was experimenting with light and radiation. He didn't know what they were. So, he named them "X"-ray, meaning "unknown."

Magnetic resonance imaging (MRI) scanners also allow doctors to look inside a person's body. The first full-body MRI scanner was built in 1977. Since then, MRIs have become faster, stronger, and more accurate. MRIs, like the one below, use magnets and a computer program to take pictures of the soft parts of a human body. Doctors use the images to diagnose, or identify, what is causing someone pain.

High-tech View
Mixed-reality glasses, a type of VR technology, are a new way for doctors to "see" inside a body. During surgery, doctors can use their voice or hand motions to access a patient's records and see 3D models of the person's body.

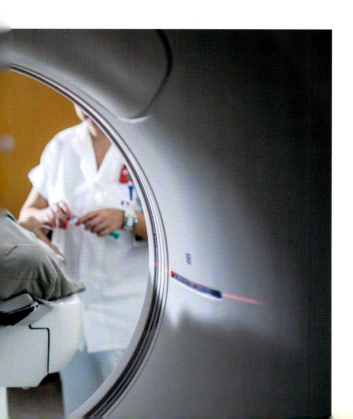

Mighty Magnets
The magnets in an MRI are 3,000 times stronger than a refrigerator magnet.

31

Telehealth Limits
Sometimes, it's not possible to have a telehealth visit with the doctor. X-rays, blood work, and some examinations must be done in person for the doctor to make an accurate diagnosis.

Some medical technologies simply make life easier and healthier for everyone. Telehealth visits are a great example. Instead of going to a doctor's office, patients can stay home and visit with healthcare providers on the phone or online.

Telehealth visits became popular during the COVID-19 pandemic. These visits helped slow the spread of the virus. They are also good options when illness, distance, or busy schedules prevent patients from traveling to a doctor's office.

Wearable medical devices also help people stay healthy. Some wearable devices are made for people with specific medical needs. They track important data like blood sugar levels and heart rate. They send that information to a doctor.

Smart watches are a type of wearable medical device. They track the amount of exercise and sleep a person gets each day. This helps people make decisions about their health. They can also play music during a workouts and be programmed to alert someone when they've been sitting for too long!

Monitoring Diabetes
Bodies turn food into sugar to use for energy. Diabetes affects the way bodies use sugar. People with diabetes must check their glucose, or blood sugar, level regularly to make sure it doesn't get too high or too low. Glucose monitoring devices stick to a person's arm and measure their blood sugar level every five minutes.

Seedling Controversy
Some people believe GM seeds could help solve one of the greatest challenges of the 21st century—world hunger. Others fear that plants grown from GM seeds will compete with native species and have a negative impact on biodiversity. Biodiversity is all the different plant and animal species that live in an area.

AGRICULTURAL TECHNOLOGY

Technology also improves the way people grow food. Scientists have created genetically modified (GM) seeds for plants that resist insects, drought, viruses, and diseases. The seeds help farmers grow more productive crops.

Satellites also help. Satellites collect data on temperature, moisture, and everything else that can affect how plants grow. Some parts of a farm are wetter or weedier than other parts. Farmers use the data they collect to make sure plants in each area get the resources they need to grow well.

This process is called precision farming. It helps protect the environment and keeps food prices down.

Let's not forget equipment. Modern tractors have been able to steer themselves for many years, but a person still had to be on the tractor. But in recent years, agricultural equipment companies have taken that technology further. There's even a tractor that can drive itself! Farmers can control it with a cell phone.

Filling a Gap
Many young people raised on farms move to cities, so farm workers are in short supply. Driverless tractors may help solve that labor shortage so farmers can produce enough food to feed the world.

35

Cow ID
Ranchers and dairy farmers use electronic identification tags (EID) to track information about their cattle. EID tags are small, button-like computer chips that attach to an animal's ear. When scanned, the tags bring up all the stored information about the animal—from its birth date to its health history.

Technology helps those who raise animals, too. Some ranches are huge, so ranchers use drones to keep an eye on everything. As a drone flies over, the rancher can see how much water and grass are available. If there is not enough, it's time to move cattle to a different pasture.

Drones have other uses, too. Ranchers can use a drone's heat-sensing cameras to find missing cattle—even if they are standing in canyons or under trees.

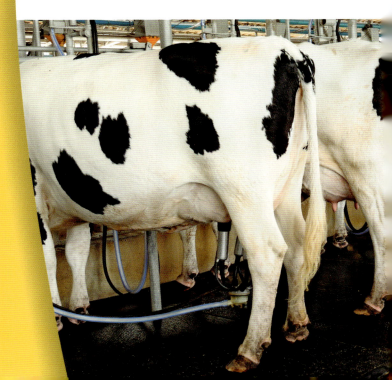

Some dairy farmers use robotic milking systems. Each cow has an electronic tag. The robot reads the tag and identifies the cow. It supplies the correct amount and type of food for that cow.

As a cow eats, the robot washes its udders and attaches the milking cups. A computer tracks how much milk is produced and how much food the cow has eaten. After milking, everything is washed and ready for the next cow.

Robot Chores
Milking cows isn't the only thing robots can do on a farm. There are also robots that feed cows, scrape up manure, and keep barns tidy.

Making Milk
Many cows produce up to 12 gallons (45 liters) of milk a day. That's enough milk to make five pounds (2.3 kg) of butter, 12 pounds (5.4 kg) of mozzarella cheese, or eight gallons (30 liters) of ice cream!

37

Electric Bikes
There are electric bikes, too! E-bikes are slightly larger than regular bikes and run on an electric battery. They help people pedal and can go up to 28 miles per hour (45 kph)!

Magnetic Elevator
A multi-directional elevator also uses magnet technology. Instead of ropes and cables pulling the elevator up, magnets push and pull the elevator up, down—and side to side!

TECHNOLOGY AND TRANSPORTATION

Transportation technologies improve how people and cargo move around town or across the country. Currently, most vehicles are powered with fossil fuels like oil and natural gas. These kinds of fuels take a long time to form naturally. So, researchers searched for new ways to power vehicles.

Electric cars have been around for many years. Better batteries have made it possible for these vehicles to travel up to 400 miles (645 km) before needing to be recharged.

Magnets are another way to power vehicles. The first magnetic levitation (maglev) train opened in 1984. Maglev uses magnets to "float" a train above its tracks. One set of magnets pushes the train up. Another set pushes it forward.

Today, researchers are using maglev technology to develop a new kind of transportation called a hyperloop. A hyperloop uses magnets to push train-like pods through a sealed tube. The pod uses very little energy and can move faster than most airplanes can fly.

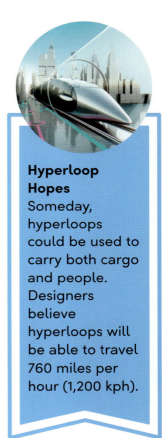

Hyperloop Hopes
Someday, hyperloops could be used to carry both cargo and people. Designers believe hyperloops will be able to travel 760 miles per hour (1,200 kph).

Shanghai Maglev Train

Seeing in the Dark
Night vision cameras let drivers see what's hiding in the dark.

No Talking Zone
Automobiles now have technology that can put cell phones on silent while people are driving. This helps drivers stay focused on the road.

Engineers regularly develop new technologies that make vehicles safer. New cars have sensors that warn drivers when an object is in their path or another car is too close. If the driver doesn't respond, the car automatically brakes.

Some new cars come equipped with night vision. These cars use thermal imaging cameras to help drivers see better in the dark.

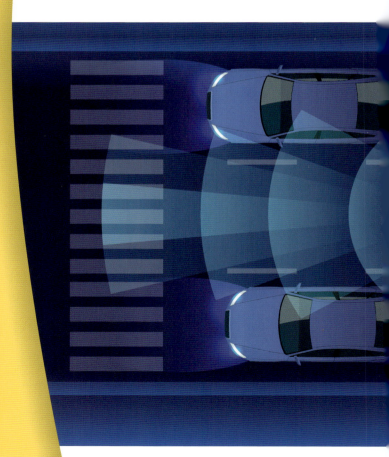

Other safety ideas are still in development. For instance, engineers want to put sensors in a driver's seatbelt or gearshift that recognize when the driver isn't focused enough to drive. The sensors would trigger the car's computer to turn off the car before the driver accidently hurt someone.

Time Out! People get tired when they drive long distances. But driving long distances is part of the job for truck drivers who haul freight across the country. To help them stay safe and alert on the road, there are laws that say when truck drivers should take breaks and how long they can drive in one day.

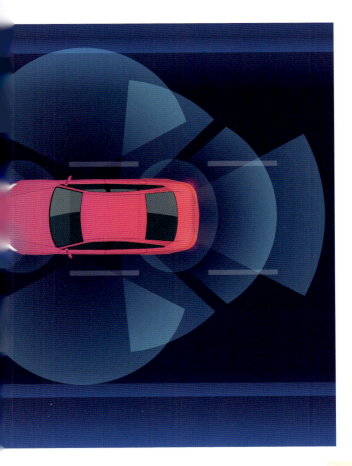

41

Exploring Space
In 2021, a space rover named Perseverance and a mini robotic helicopter called Ingenuity set down on Mars. What their experiments uncover may pave the way for humans to someday travel to Mars.

EXPLORING WITH TECHNOLOGY

Humans can't dive deep into the ocean unless they are in a submarine. The pressure and cold are too extreme. We can't walk on the Moon without protection either. The atmosphere would kill us. But we still know a lot about the ocean and Moon thanks to technology. Humans have used technology to explore the world around us for centuries.

Today, we learn a lot from robots. Robots can go places humans cannot. One of the most famous scientific robots is exploring the planet Mars right now. Curiosity is a space rover. Its robotic arms collect rock and dirt samples from the surface of the Red Planet. Its sensors and cameras operate like a science laboratory on wheels. Curiosity sends all the data it collects back to scientists on Earth.

Curiosity began exploring Mars in 2012. It was sent to discover whether life could have ever existed there.

Remotely operated vehicles, or ROVs, are underwater robots that explore the ocean. ROVs can dive deeper and stay underwater much longer than humans can. Onboard cameras film sea life. Sensors measure the water's depth and temperature. The data are sent through a long cable to scientists waiting on a boat. Some ROVs also collect samples.

To All Extremes
Ocean temperatures range from 28 to 86°F (−2 to 30°C). But near thermal vents, water can be as hot as 750°F (400°C)! Only an ROV could manage such extremes.

Enduring Tech
Scientists designed Curiosity to survive the harsh Martian atmosphere for at least 687 Earth days, which is one Martian year. No one expected Curiosity to be working 10 years later!

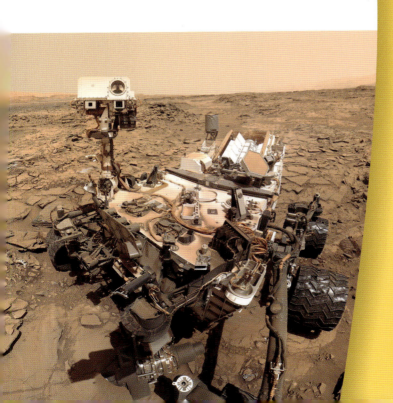

43

Changing History
Recently, archaeologists using LiDAR data uncovered the remains of a previously unknown civilization buried deep in the Amazon rainforest. Their findings have caused historians to reconsider their understanding of the history of the Amazon.

LiDAR
LiDAR can be used to map buildings and cities. It can also see through shallow ocean water to create maps of coastlines.

Many places on Earth are also hard for humans to explore. Some places are too dangerous. Others are hard to get to or difficult to travel through. But that doesn't mean they are impossible to study—not when technology can help.

Imagine a rainforest. Sometimes, scientists backpack through the jungle, recording data and taking samples by hand. Other times, they study rainforests from above. They use Light Detection and Ranging (LiDAR) technology. LiDAR is strong enough to see through the tree canopy to create a detailed map of the rainforest floor.

How does LiDAR work? As an airplane flies over an area, LiDAR uses a laser to send pulses of light toward the ground. The light bounces back to the airplane, and LiDAR records the data. It then uses GPS technology to measure the distance from the airplane to each object it detected to create a map.

Technology touches every part of our lives. It makes our lives easier. It makes us more productive and helps us learn. As long as people keep creating new kinds of technology, the possibilities of what we can do are endless.

Seeing Below
Ground-penetrating radar (GPR) is another type of technology that lets people see underground. GPR sends radio waves into the ground. The waves bounce back when they encounter different materials. Sensors read that data, and the GPR creates a map of objects hidden below the surface.

45

GLOSSARY

Code
A set of instructions for a computer

Collaborate
To work with others

Communicate
To transmit information

Drone
An aircraft or ship with no pilot that is controlled by remote control

Electromagnetic waves
Waves of energy produced by electric and magnetic fields

Fossil fuels
Fuels such as coal, oil, and natural gas made from the remains (fossils) of plants and animals

GPS
A navigation system that uses satellites to find locations on Earth

Network
A group of connected objects, like computers, that share information

Open-source
Computer software code that is freely available and can be easily used or changed

Podcast
A digital program that can be downloaded or streamed from the internet

Rover
A vehicle that explores the surface of space objects, such as the moon

Stream
To transfer digital data in a continuous flow that can be played back immediately

Technology
The practical use of scientific knowledge

Virtual reality
An artificial environment created by a computer that resembles the real world through sight and sound

World Wide Web
The system that links together the information on the internet

INDEX

agricultural technology 34–37

archaeology 44

automobiles 38, 40–41

barcodes 23

bikes, electric 38

binary code 11

Bluetooth 21

businesses 22–25

cars 38, 40–41

cattle 36–37

communication 8–15

computers 7, 11, 23–25, 37
see also internet

Curiosity rover 42, 43

diabetes 33

drones 36

electric cars 38

electronic identification tags (EID) 36, 37

elevator, magnetic 38

email 12, 13

entertainment 16–21

exploration 42–45

fake news 18, 19

farming 34–37

genetically modified (GM) seeds 34

GPS 28, 45

ground-penetrating radar (GPR) 45

Hertz, Heinrich 8–9

home technology 26–27

hospitals 28–33

hyperloops 39

internet
about 12–15

news and entertainment 17–19

online shopping 22

search engines 14

smart devices 20

telecommuting 23

virtual assistants 27

Internet of Things (IoT) 20

King, Ada (countess of Lovelace) 7

LiDAR (Light Detection and Ranging) 44–45

light bulbs 27

magnetic levitation (maglev) trains 39

magnetic resonance imaging (MRI) 31

Mars rovers 42, 43

medical technology 28–33

Morse code 8

movies 16

nanobots 29

NASA (National Aeronautics and Space Administration) 9, 13

news and entertainment 16–21

newspapers 16, 17

night vision cameras 40

ocean exploration 42, 43

open-source technologies 19

phones
agricultural technology 35
automobile technology 40
history 9

news alerts 16

virtual assistants 27

wireless technology 10, 11

podcasts 18

QR codes 22, 23

radio waves 8–9, 11, 13

remotely operated vehicles (ROVs) 43

robots 25–29, 37, 42

Roentgen, Wilhelm 30

rovers 42, 43

schools 24–25

search engines 14

Smart TVs 20–21

smart watches 33

space exploration 42

stores 22–23

technology, definition of 6

telecommuting 23

telegraphs 8, 9

telehealth visits 32

television 16, 17, 20–21

Tomlinson, Ray 13

tractors 35

transportation 38–41

truck drivers 41

virtual assistants 26, 27

virtual classrooms 24–25

virtual reality (VR) 21, 28, 31

wearable medical devices 33

Wi-Fi 13, 20

work and school 22–25

World Wide Web 15

X-rays 30

47

QUIZ

Answer the questions to see what you have learned. Check your answers in the key below.

1. What is technology?

2. What do wireless devices like cell phones use to send and receive information?

3. True or False: Everything you read on the internet is accurate.

4. What do barcodes and QR codes do?

5. What does an MRI use to take pictures of your body?

6. Why did engineers create genetically modified seeds?

7. What makes maglev trains "float" above their tracks?

8. What kind of technology helps scientists explore the ocean?

1. The practical use of science 2. Radio waves 3. False
4. Store information about products 5. Magnets and a computer program 6. To have seeds that can resist insects, drought, viruses, and diseases 7. Magnets 8. Remotely operated vehicles (ROVs)